THROUGH
LIFE'S
STORMS

From Heartbreak to Healing:
Learning to Live Again After Loss

GENEVA HUDSON

www.TrueVinePublishing.org

Through Life's Storms
Geneva Hudson

Published by
True Vine Publishing Co.
810 Dominican Dr.
Nashville, TN 37228
www.TrueVinePublishing.org

DEDICATION

I dedicate this book to my daughter Christy L. Hudson and my wonderful grandchildren.

TABLE OF CONTENTS

INTRODUCTION

There are moments in life that change everything, even if you do not understand them at first. Moments that feel small when they happen but later reveal themselves as turning points. Sometimes the storm does not announce itself with thunder. Sometimes it begins with a shift in someone's eyes. A silence that lingers too long. A conversation you do not realize is your last normal one.

Storms rarely send invitations. They simply arrive. This book was not written because I wanted to become an author. It was written because I survived things I did not think I could survive. It was written because I discovered that pain, if left unspoken, grows heavier, and sometimes the only way to breathe again is to tell the truth about what took your breath away.

I have known poverty. I have known abuse. I have known what it feels like to start over with nothing but determination and prayer. I have learned what it means to stretch a little food into a meal, to stretch a little money into a week, and to stretch a little strength into another day. I have learned how to keep moving while my heart begged me to sit down.

I have worked long hours. I have raised children without help. I have faced moments when I did not know how I would make it through another day. And I have learned that strength is not loud. Sometimes strength is simply getting up when you would rather stay down. Sometimes it is brushing your teeth when you do not feel like looking in the mirror. Sometimes it is putting clothes on your child while your own spirit feels tired. Sometimes it is choosing to keep living when you are not sure how.

This book is not about perfection. It is not about having all the answers. It is about learning in real time. It is about watching closely. Listening deeply. Loving intentionally. It is about the reality that our children grow into their own minds, their own pressures, their own battles, and sometimes those battles are silent. It is also about the way storms can make you pay attention to what you used to overlook, and how wisdom often comes after you have already needed it.

As you read these pages, you will find honesty. You will find warning signs that are easy to overlook. You will find reflections that may sound familiar to your own home, your own family, your own heart. You will find the reminder that even when life shifts suddenly, your story is not finished. You will also find reminders that love is not only a feeling, it is an action, and sometimes the most powerful thing you can do is stay present and stay willing to see what is really happening.

You will also find faith; not the kind that pretends everything is fine, but the kind that holds on when nothing makes sense. You will find resilience as a daily decision. You will see what it looks like to keep standing when standing feels unnatural. You will see that survival does not always look like a breakthrough. Sometimes it looks like consistency. It looks like showing up again. It looks like doing the next right thing even when your heart feels heavy.

If you are a parent, this book will help you look closer and love louder. It will help you understand that asking questions is not being nosy, it is being responsible. It will help you create room for your child to be honest, even when the truth is uncomfortable. If you are grieving, this book will give language to emotions that feel impossible to explain. If you are walking through something heavy and silent, this book will remind you that you are not weak for feeling it, and you are not alone for carrying it.

My prayer is that these pages give you awareness where there was once assumption, courage where there was once fear, and hope where there was once confusion. Storms may come, but so can wisdom, clarity, and strength; and sometimes, the very story that almost broke you becomes the one that helps someone else stand.

Let's begin.

SECTION I

UNDERSTANDING THE STORM

CHAPTER 1

The First Storm I Survived

I married very young. I was not allowed to date, so in my mind, marriage felt like the only way to have a boyfriend. Instead of learning life, I stepped straight into being someone's wife before I even learned who I was. I did not understand what I needed. I did not understand what I deserved. I just knew I wanted to feel chosen, and I thought marriage meant love would automatically be safe.

From the beginning, the marriage was rough. He drank often, smoked constantly, and carried jealousy like a shadow. I did not drink or smoke, and I could feel the distance between our lives every time he lit a cigarette or came home smelling like alcohol. It was not just the smell. It was the attitude that came with it, like the alcohol made him feel entitled to control the air in the room. Arguments, fist fights, and all-out brawls came easily. The smallest thing could turn into a storm.

"Why are you speaking to him?" he would snap if a man held a door open for me at the store.

"I was being polite," I would say, trying to keep the peace.

"Don't play with me," he would answer, convinced something was going on that never existed.

Jealousy does not need proof. It only needs a target. It made him listen to his own imagination more than he listened to me. It made him punish me for things that never happened. It made me start shrinking without realizing it. I would watch my words, measure my tone, and plan my answers before questions even came, just trying to avoid the next explosion.

If he quit a job, I encouraged him to get another one. That led to more fighting. I wasn't trying to embarrass him. I was trying to keep the lights on, keep food in the house, keep diapers and shoes on the children. But anything that sounded like responsibility made him angry, and any anger he carried, he brought home to me. It was like walking on cracked glass every day, hoping nothing sharp pushed through the floor. I learned how to clean up messes fast and pretend everything was normal, because I did not want the outside world to know how we lived inside our walls.

I stayed because of my children. I had two boys and one girl. I wanted them to have a father in the house, even if the house never felt peaceful. I kept believing he would change. I figured I could hold everything together long enough for something to get better. But the fights grew harder, the tension heavier, and I realized my children were watching everything. They were learning what love looked like through fear. They were learning what a woman should accept, what a man was allowed to do, and what silence was supposed to cover. That broke me.

I noticed it in small moments first. The way my children got quiet when his car pulled up. The way they listened for his footsteps, the way they watched his face for signs, the way they tried to disappear when he got loud. Children learn survival early when they live in chaos. Their bodies will tell the truth even when their mouths do not. My house had become a place where everybody was always bracing for something. That is not a home. That is a storm shelter.

When he slammed the door one night to go drinking after another fight, something inside me cracked open. The yelling still echoed in the walls, and the children were still shaking from it. I stood in the middle of that small room, breathing hard, telling myself, "This is it. You leave tonight." I was tired of apologizing for things I did not do. I was tired of living like I needed permission to exist. I was tired of watching my children carry fear on their faces.

My hands were shaking as I grabbed whatever I could reach: a couple of shirts, a blanket, one bag that barely zipped. My daughter whispered, "Mama, where we going?" I didn't answer. Not because I didn't want to, but because I truly didn't know. That is what faith looks like sometimes. You move without a map. You move because staying is more dangerous than not knowing.

I took each child by the hand and walked out into the night. The air was cool, almost cold, and the neighborhood streetlights flickered like they were struggling to stay alive. My son cried, wiping his face with his sleeve, his little voice breaking as he said he was scared. My heart was scared too, but I could not afford to let them feel that.

"Mama's right here," I kept saying, even though fear was twisting in my own chest. My feet hurt as if I had rocks inside my shoes, but I kept going. Stopping meant going back, and going back meant dying slowly inside the life I had just escaped. I kept telling myself that I did not have to know the whole plan. I just had to take the next step.

We walked until the houses thinned out and the streets got quieter. The sound of dogs barking in the distance mixed with the hum of passing cars. My middle child clung to my leg, whispering, "I'm tired."

My oldest tried to be brave, helping carry the bag, even though his arms were trembling. I kept looking around, trying to find anywhere we could rest. A porch. A shed. A stairwell. Something.

Then I saw it: a dark shape sitting back behind overgrown bushes. At first glance, it didn't even look like a house. Just a structure swallowed by weeds. No lights. No curtains. The fence next to it leaned so far it looked like a breath would knock it over. Every part of it gave off a chill, like the kind of place children dare each other to go near during the day. But the darkness had its own kind of mercy. No one yelling. No one following. No one watching.

"Stay close," I whispered, pulling my kids toward the yard.

As we approached, I could smell the damp wood. The house felt cold even from the outside, like time had settled over it. I tried the back door. Locked. The front door. Locked. My heart dropped into my stomach.

My daughter started crying again. "Mama, please… let's go back home?"

"We gon' be alright," I said, with a steady voice, but shaky heart.

I walked around the side and ran my fingers along the boards covering the windows. One of them was loose. The nails barely held on. I pushed. The board groaned but didn't move. I pushed harder, using my whole body, until it finally snapped free and fell into the darkness inside.

"Mama?"

"It's okay," I said. "Help your brother through."

I lifted them one by one through the opening. Their small legs scraped against the wood, and they landed inside with soft thuds. When it was my turn, I crawled in slowly, brushing cobwebs away with my forearm. The air inside smelled like dust, old paper, and wood that had been left too long in the humidity. I stood up and listened. Nothing. No footsteps overhead. No voices. No movement. Just stillness.

I kept my hands stretched out in front of me, feeling my way around. The floor creaked under each step, and the children huddled close, grabbing the sides of my shirt. Their breathing was fast and uneven. My own breathing was loud in my ears. I remember thinking how strange it was that an empty house could still feel like it was judging you, like it knew you did not belong there.

Then my fingers brushed against a wall. Cold. Rough. But solid. I found a corner and spread the thin blanket across the floor. "Sit here," I told the kids. My youngest crawled into my lap, face still wet from tears. My sons lay beside me, one arm over my waist as if he was trying to protect me the same way I protected him.

For the first time in a long time, the night was quiet. There were no slammed doors, no footsteps storming down the hallway, no cursing, no shattering glass, no fear waiting for me in the next room. We were sitting in darkness, on a dusty wooden floor inside an abandoned house, but the quiet felt like safety. For the first time in years, I could breathe without waiting for something bad to happen. I pressed my cheek against my son's head and whispered, "We're safe tonight."

The wind whistled through the broken window. The smell of dust filled my nose. The floor groaned beneath us. My heart was still racing, but slowly, slowly, it settled. The children's breathing became softer. Their bodies relaxed against mine.

We did not know what tomorrow would bring, but for that moment, sitting there in the dark, tired feet finally resting on the floor of a house that was not ours, we had peace. And peace was enough for one night.

Leaving that night taught me something I did not understand while I was living in the chaos. Strength does not always look like fighting back. Sometimes, strength is picking up your babies with shaking hands and walking into the unknown because staying would break you. Sometimes strength is a whispered "We gon' be alright" when you do not have a plan, only faith. That night showed me that survival is not always loud or confident. It is often quiet, trembling, and desperate. But it is still survival. And if you can take one step toward peace, even through a broken window in the dark, God will meet you there.

CHAPTER 2

Living in the Shadows

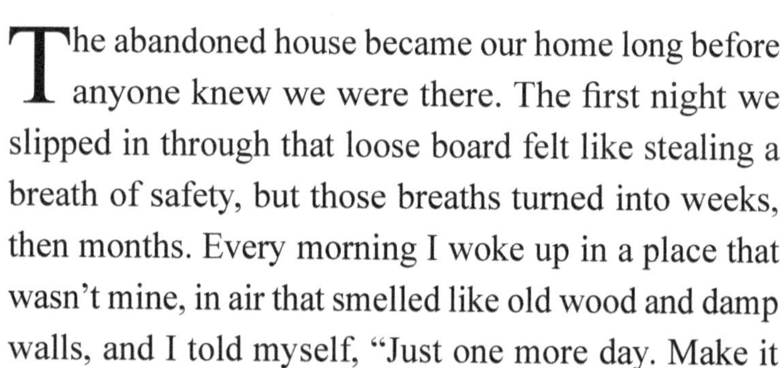

The abandoned house became our home long before anyone knew we were there. The first night we slipped in through that loose board felt like stealing a breath of safety, but those breaths turned into weeks, then months. Every morning I woke up in a place that wasn't mine, in air that smelled like old wood and damp walls, and I told myself, "Just one more day. Make it through one more day."

In the daytime, the house looked different than it did at night. The darkness made it feel like a hiding place, but the daylight exposed everything. Sunlight slid through the cracks in the boards like thin fingers, landing on dusty floors and peeling paint. The silence wasn't peaceful. It was cautious. The kind of quiet you keep when you're trying not to be found.

The children always woke up before me, their whispers breaking the stillness. I would open my eyes and see them sitting up, blankets pulled tight, hair messy from sleeping on hard boards. "Mama, you up?" they would ask, touching my arm gently as if they were checking to make sure I was still there. I forced a smile even when my body felt heavy. "Yeah, baby, I'm up. Come on, let's get moving." I learned how to sound steady even when I didn't feel steady.

We had no lights, so the mornings started with gray daylight creeping in. I would count what we had before I did anything else. Food. Water. Clean clothes. Time. I didn't realize then how much time I spent measuring life in small pieces, like survival came in teaspoons. When you are living in the shadows, you don't plan weeks ahead. You plan the next hour.

The water situation was the hardest. No matter what we had, we needed water. I found a nearby gas station with an outside spigot, and I learned the best time to use it was early, before anyone paid attention. I would carry an old milk jug and fill it over and over, the plastic cold against my fingers. Some mornings the water hit my hands like ice, and I would flinch but keep going. I wasn't just filling a jug. I was filling a chance.

I used that water to wash their faces and brush their teeth, trying to make them feel normal. I learned how to wash dishes with barely anything. I learned how to stretch a little water like it was gold. I did not want my children to feel like we were living like animals. I wanted them to still feel like children, even in a place that wasn't meant for anyone.

Food was whatever I could afford and whatever I could bring home. Cereal with no milk. Sandwiches when we had bread. Fast food from my job when the manager let me take leftovers. Some nights the smell of grease clung to my uniform when I hugged them, and they pressed their faces into my shirt like the smell itself was comfort. I watched them chew slowly, like they were trying to make the meal last, and that hurt me more than hunger did.

Work kept us alive. I got a job at a fast-food restaurant near the bus line so I could reach it without walking too far in the dark. Every morning, I left before sunrise. That part never got easier. I would stand at the door, look at their faces, and feel the guilt rise up in my throat. They were too young to be alone, but I was too desperate to quit.

Before I walked out, I would give instructions like I was training them for war. Stay inside. Don't open the door. Don't answer nobody. Don't argue with each other. I tried to make it sound like rules, but really it was fear talking. I would lock them in, then place my hand on the door for a few seconds and whisper, "Lord, cover them." Some days I prayed quietly. Some days I prayed with tears already sitting in my eyes.

Catching the bus meant stepping into the morning chill while the streets were still empty. The sky still held onto the last of the night, and every shadow felt like a threat. I would walk fast, head down, listening to dogs bark or cars hiss by, hoping no one asked me why I was out so early or why my clothes carried the faint smell of a place we were hiding in. On the bus, I stared out the window, tapping my foot, rehearsing every possible scenario in my head. What if they got scared? What if somebody knocked? What if a neighbor noticed? What if they walked outside looking for me?

At work, I moved like a machine because machines don't have time to fall apart. Take orders. Drop fries. Wipe counters. Smile when customers complain. My hands worked, but my mind was back at that house. The pressure sat on my chest like a weight I carried every shift. When my manager raised his voice over kitchen noise, it made my stomach tighten, because loud voices still sounded like danger to me. Even the beeping timers and clanging trays felt like they were shouting.

When my shift ended, I ran for the bus like my life depended on it, because it did. The whole ride back, my eyes stayed on the road, willing the driver to go faster. I imagined the children sitting on that floor waiting for the sound of my steps. Every stoplight felt personal, like the world was slowing me down on purpose. I was holding myself together with one thought: get back to them.

Every time I pushed open that loose back door, the relief hit me like a wave. There they were. Three little faces lifting at the same time. "Mama's home." Their trust in me made everything feel heavier and lighter at the same time. Heavier because I knew I couldn't fail them, and lighter because they were still safe.

We built routines inside that abandoned house the way people build routines in real homes, except ours were shaped by hiding. I taught them to whisper after dark. I taught them not to stomp on the floorboards. I taught them to keep the windows covered. I swept the floors with a piece of cardboard, pushing dust into piles just to feel like the place belonged to us. We spread blankets along the wall where the boards let in the least wind. At night, I lay between them, listening for footsteps outside, for car doors, for anything that sounded off. My ears never fully rested. Even in sleep, I stayed alert.

Still, we survived. The children found ways to be children, because that is what children do. They drew pictures on scraps of paper and taped them to the walls so the rooms didn't feel so empty. My daughter would hum to herself while she played, like she was trying to create music where there was none. My boys played with sticks they found in the yard like they were swords, chasing each other and laughing quietly. Those small sounds of life felt like proof that we weren't defeated.

Months passed. Long enough for seasons to shift. Long enough for the wind to change direction and sneak in through cracks like an uninvited guest. Long enough for my children to stop asking when we were going home, because this was home now. That realization hit me one night when my youngest pointed to a corner of the room and called it "our spot." My throat tightened because I knew what it meant. They were settling into something that was never supposed to be permanent.

Then one afternoon, everything changed.

I had just returned from work, and the kids were outside playing in the yard, picking up rocks and giggling about some secret game. I was inside setting down my purse when I heard a car pull up. The engine clicked off. Doors shut. I stepped toward the window, careful not to move the board too much, and saw a man walking toward them.

His boots crunched over fallen branches. The children froze, like they felt the danger before they understood it. He stood there looking at them, then looking at the house behind them. His face wasn't angry at first, just confused, like he was trying to make sense of what he was seeing.

"Who are y'all?" he asked, voice steady. "Why are you here?"

The kids didn't answer. My daughter's voice shook when she whispered, "Mama," and pointed toward him.

I stepped onto the porch with my heart racing so hard it felt like it was trying to climb out of my chest. "Can I help you?" I asked, even though my voice sounded smaller than I wanted it to.

He looked at me, then at the children, then back at the house. "This house belongs to my family," he said.

My stomach dropped. It felt like all the air left my chest at once. I expected him to curse. I expected him to threaten me. I expected the end of the little shelter I had built out of desperation. Instead, I swallowed and told the truth, because there wasn't anything else to tell.

"I know," I said quietly. "I had nowhere else to go."

For a moment, he didn't say a word. He just stared at me, taking everything in. The children's thin clothes. Their bare feet. The patched blankets hanging in the window. My tired face. My worn-out shoes. He saw the truth written all over us. I braced myself, waiting for him to tell me to get out, to leave, to take my babies and step back into the night we barely survived.

Instead, he let out a long breath. "Let me talk to my people," he said.

When he drove away, I stood there shaking, not sure if that sentence was mercy or a warning. That night, I barely slept. Every sound made me sit up. Every car that passed made my heart jump. I kept thinking, what if they come tomorrow and put us out? Where will I take them? How far can I walk with three children and one bag again?

The next day he came back, and he wasn't alone. He brought relatives. Men and women. People with eyes that looked like they had lived life. I stood at the doorway gripping the sides of my shirt, my body already preparing for shame, because being seen in your struggle feels like being exposed.

They walked through the rooms slowly, their footsteps echoing in the hollow halls. They looked at places where I had swept dust away. They traced the drawings the children had taped to the wall. They examined the corner where we slept. They didn't see criminals. They saw a mother trying.

One of the women said softly, "Lord have mercy."

Another man shook his head. "These babies been living like this?"

I wanted to shrink, but before I could speak, the man who owned the house said, "We gotta help her." He didn't say it like a favor. He said it like a decision.

And they did.

They brought materials and started repairing what had been broken for a long time. They patched sheetrock. They replaced boards. They sealed cracks that let wind cut through the rooms. They cleared out old trash and broken glass and made space for us to breathe. When water finally ran, I stood at the sink and cried quietly so my children wouldn't see. When lights came on, the house didn't just look different, it felt different. The shadows didn't hold us the same way anymore.

They didn't ask me for money upfront. They didn't make me beg. After they made the home livable, they only asked for a small amount each month. I can only assume it helped pay for electricity and water, but even if it didn't, it was still mercy. It was still a way forward.

With stability came a different kind of hope. I opened a small daycare, keeping other people's children along with my own. The sound of laughter filled rooms that once echoed with emptiness. I sold newspaper subscriptions. I cleaned houses. I took whatever work came because survival had a price, and I was willing to pay it. I wasn't just trying to live. I was trying to climb.

I learned that a woman can rise from places she was never meant to stay. I learned that strength comes in whispers, not shouts. I learned that sometimes help comes from strangers, and sometimes God tucks a blessing inside an abandoned house. I also learned that pride can kill you if you let it. If I had let shame silence me, I would have stayed trapped. But I kept showing up. I kept working. I kept praying. I kept mothering. I kept moving.

We lived in the shadows for a long time, but little by little, life came back to us, one repaired board, one paycheck, one prayer at a time. Day by day, I was becoming someone stronger than the girl who ran away. I was becoming a woman who could stand.

CHAPTER 3

A Different Kind of Love

After you have lived through yelling, jealousy, and fists, peace does not feel peaceful at first. It feels suspicious. It feels like a setup. It feels like the calm before another explosion. That is where my heart was when I met him. I did not trust anyone enough to let them get close, and I did not trust myself enough to recognize something healthy when it showed up.

By then, I had learned how to survive. I had learned how to work, how to protect my children, how to keep my head down and keep moving. But surviving and healing are not the same thing. I was functioning, but I was still guarded. My heart had armor on it, and I had convinced myself that armor was wisdom.

I was walking to the laundromat with my children like I did every weekend. Bags tugged at my arms, detergent pressed cold against my palm, and my feet kept the same steady rhythm because stopping meant getting noticed. Cars slowed down beside us sometimes. Men would offer rides like it was nothing. I learned to keep my eyes forward, my answers short, and my children close. When you are a single woman walking with three children, you feel seen in a way that is not always safe.

That day, another car slowed down, matching our pace. The window rolled down, and I tightened my grip on the laundry bags without thinking. The man behind the wheel was big, about five eleven, broad in his shoulders, dark brown skin, mustache and beard, and brown eyes that held steady when they met mine. His name was Winston. His voice was deep, rough like gravel, but calm.

Winston asked questions like he already expected an answer. "Are you married?" "Do you have a boyfriend?" "Can I get to know you?"

I stopped walking and faced him because I did not like being talked to from the side of a moving car. "Why are you asking me all that?" I said, and he smiled like my attitude did not scare him. I asked if he was married because I was not about to be anybody's secret, and he said no.

I told him I had three children, and he said he could see that. He asked for my number, and I laughed because life had me walking to the laundromat with bottles and bags. "I don't have a phone," I said, and his face did not change. He asked where I lived and offered to take us home. I told him no. He offered to put our things in the car. I told him no again.

He followed us to the laundromat anyway, still talking, still trying. I felt irritation and fear rising at the same time. Persistence can feel romantic in movies. In real life, when you have lived through control, it feels like danger. I turned on him right there between the washers and dryers.

"Today is not the day. Leave me alone."

He lifted his hands like he was backing off, but the look he gave me stuck with me. It wasn't angry. It wasn't offended. It was serious, like he meant what he said but wasn't going to force it. That was different. Most men would have cursed or insulted me. He didn't.

The next week, I caught myself hoping he would not show up. That is how I knew he had gotten under my skin. I didn't like that. I was tired of being approached, tired of being watched, tired of men acting like my life was open for discussion. I wanted to disappear into my responsibilities and not feel noticed by anybody.

Then I saw him again, not even at the laundromat. I was walking out of the yard, headed toward the store, and his car passed, then circled back. He told me I looked like I had a husband. I almost laughed at that. I had been through marriage. I knew what it cost.

He said he was not there to hurt me. He said he was there to help me. I did not believe that easily. Help had strings attached in my experience. Help had expectations. Help had moods that could shift. I told him I would think about dinner, but I did not promise him anything.

When I finally said yes, the dinner was not fancy, but it was calm. That is what I noticed first. Calm. He did not try to impress me with money or bragging. He did not try to dominate the conversation. He asked my children questions like they mattered. He looked them in the eyes. He spoke to them with respect. They warmed up faster than I did, laughing and eating like they could sense something safe before I could.

I kept watching him, waiting for something ugly to slip out. Waiting for the tone to change. Waiting for control to show up. Trauma makes you study people like they are puzzles.

When he brought us home, I did not invite him in. I told him I was taking the kids inside and would come back out. When I stepped back outside, he moved toward me like he had earned something. He grabbed me and tried to kiss me, and my whole body snapped back.

"Hold up," I said. "You bought one dinner. Don't act like you got the whole house open."

My voice was sharp, and I meant it. I told him he was moving too fast and to get out of my yard. I was ready for anger. I was ready for ego. I was ready for insults.

He didn't curse. He didn't argue. He didn't call me names. He stepped back and said he could treat me like a lady if I would stop fighting him. Then he left.

That moment mattered more than I realized at the time. He respected my no. That is something abuse does not prepare you for. When you have lived through control, you expect resistance to your boundaries. You expect punishment for them. When he left calmly, something inside me shifted a little.

Three days later, he pulled up in my yard with a car. He had keys in his hand. He said no more walking down the street with bottles and bags. No more dragging babies along the roadside like life did not see us.

I stared at him, waiting for the catch. Waiting for the "but." Waiting for the moment he would use that gift against me. I had learned to expect debt where generosity was offered.

He never came back to take it. He never held it over my head. That gift did not feel romantic at first. It felt dangerous. I did not know how to receive something without owing something. But we needed it. My children needed it.

After that, he proved himself in quiet ways. If the car broke down, he came. If something in the house needed fixing, he showed up and fixed it without making me feel small. He did not talk down to me. He did not belittle me for not knowing something.

One time, I was stuck on the freeway after getting my eyes checked. My vision was blurry, and I was crying because I could not see clearly enough to feel safe driving. I called him, embarrassed and frustrated. He came like it was normal. No complaining. No lecturing. Just presence.

He did what he said he would do every time. That kind of consistency heals places you didn't know were wounded. He was older than me by about fifteen years, and he carried himself like a man who had already learned what chaos costs. He didn't compete with me. He partnered with me.

Still, I fought it. I noticed the difference right away, but I did not believe it would last. My mind kept whispering, "All men are the same." So I watched him closely. I tested him without calling it a test. I paid attention to how he handled disagreement. I paid attention to whether his tone shifted when he was tired. I paid attention to how he treated my children when they weren't listening.

He talked to me, not at me. He didn't raise his voice to feel powerful. He didn't use silence as punishment. When I made mistakes or felt embarrassed, he did not shame me. He would say something simple and uplifting, like I just used the wrong hand, and we would keep going. That kind of steady love changes a person.

Sometimes he would look at me like he was waiting on me to admit what he already knew. He would smile and ask with his eyes, "Am I your man yet?" I would roll my eyes and keep moving because stubbornness was my armor. If I did not give him my heart, he could not break it. That is what I told myself.

Then one day, I was driving and a truth hit me so fast I almost had to pull over. I found myself thinking about him, his patience, his kindness, the way he was with my children, the way he never tried to control me. The words formed in my mind clearly: I love him.

I turned the car around and drove back to his job like my heart had grabbed the steering wheel. I walked in and told him right there. I told him I loved him, and I saw relief wash over his face like he had been holding his breath for months.

After that day, I stopped fighting the love he was trying to give me. I let myself be loved.

We were together for eight years. We never got married because I had already been married, and I did not want to do it again. I did not want to sign my life over to anybody. We lived like partners. We built routines. We laughed. We argued without tearing each other down. I kept working because I never wanted love to become my only stability.

My past tried to reach for me even then. One day, I took the children to see my ex-husband, and he started acting like I still belonged to him. When I refused, he jumped on top of my car and beat on it like he could bully me back into fear. I drove away shaking and crying. When I told Winston, he said, "You are not going by yourself anymore."

The next time, he went with me. My ex-husband got quiet when he saw him standing there. Nothing had to be said loudly. The message was clear. After that, I had no more trouble. Winston protected me without controlling me. That difference mattered.

Around year six or seven, something shifted, and it wasn't our love. It was his health. He started going to the hospital more, but he kept it private. I did not know he was diabetic. I did not know he had a heart condition. I did not know he had survived a heart attack before we met. When I found out, fear crept in quietly.

One night, I had gone out with friends. Music was loud, lights flashing, people laughing like nothing in the world could break. In the middle of it, something strange happened.

I had a vision.

I saw a woman I had never met, but I recognized her from a photo. It was Winston's mother. She had been dead long before I came into his life. In my mind, she was sitting in a chair, heavyset, wearing beige pants and a striped shirt, looking at me with a serious face. She did not speak, but the look felt like a message.

It shook me. I couldn't enjoy myself after that. I tried to dismiss it. I told myself I was tired. I told myself to stop thinking. But the uneasiness wouldn't leave. I got up and decided to go home.

On the drive, I called the house to tell him I was on my way. He didn't answer. I figured he was asleep. He worked twelve to sixteen hours a day, six days a week. He would sit on the porch waiting for me to come home. That was our routine.

I pulled into the driveway acting playful, making faces, dancing a little just to make him laugh. He was sitting on the porch like always. His eyes were open, so I thought he wasn't sleeping. I teased him as I walked up the steps.

"Why you sitting out here like that?" I joked.

He didn't respond.

I stepped closer, still thinking he was playing. I tugged at his shirt the way I always did. The moment I pulled him, his body slumped forward.

He fell into me.

His weight dropped heavy and lifeless against my chest, and my breath left my body. For a second, my mind refused to understand what my hands were feeling.

"You're not playing, are you, baby? You're not playing."

Panic hit fast and blurred everything. I screamed and ran across the street to wake the neighbor who was a nurse. She moved into action while I stood shaking like my body didn't belong to me. The ambulance came. Lights flashed. The porch that once felt like peace became a scene I never wanted.

I thank God my children were asleep when it first happened. When they woke, confusion filled their faces. I gathered them up and took them to my father's house that night. I could not stay there. I stayed with my dad about two months while I found another place for us.

Winston was a different kind of love. Losing him taught me that healthy love exists. He proved my past did not have to be my blueprint. He showed me what it looked like for a man to keep his word, to protect without controlling, to respect my boundaries, and to speak without harming.

Lesson from the Storm:

If you come out of abuse, peace will feel unfamiliar. You will test people who do not deserve it. You will push away kindness and call it caution, when really it is fear. Real love respects your no. It does not rush you. It does not use help as leverage. It shows up consistently. It protects without imprisoning. It gives you room to breathe.

Peace may feel strange at first. But strange does not mean unsafe. Learning the difference can save your life.

CHAPTER 4

What I Want Young Women to Know

There are things I wish someone had told me when I was young. Not in a sermon. Not in a lecture. Not in a way that made me feel judged. I wish someone had sat me down, looked me in the eye, and spoken plainly.

So this chapter is me doing that.

If you are a young woman reading this, or even a grown woman who still feels unsure inside, I want to talk to you the way I would talk to my own daughter.

First, love should not hurt.

Let me say that again in a way that leaves no room for confusion. Love should not hurt. It should not bruise your body. It should not shrink your voice. It should not make you afraid to speak. It should not make you check someone's mood before you breathe.

When I was young, I confused intensity with love. I thought jealousy meant he cared. I thought control meant protection. I thought loud arguments meant passion. Nobody told me that real love is steady, not explosive.

If a man isolates you from your family and friends, that is not romance. That is control. If he reads your messages without permission and says it is because he loves you, that is not love. That is insecurity. If you find yourself changing who you are to avoid making him angry, you are not in a relationship. You are in survival mode.

Pay attention to how he reacts when you say no. Does he respect it? Or does he push past it? That one answer will tell you more than flowers ever could. Another thing I wish I had understood is this: your children see everything.

You may think they are too young to notice the tension in your voice or the fear in your eyes, but they notice. They hear the tone shifts. They feel the silence after arguments. They watch how you respond to disrespect.

Children learn love by watching it. They learn what is normal by living inside it.

When they see you tolerate abuse, they may grow up thinking abuse is love. When they see you stay silent, they may grow up believing silence is strength. And when they see you leave something unhealthy, even when it is hard, they learn that courage is possible.

Leaving is not weakness.

There is a lie that says staying and enduring is proof of loyalty. That if you pray hard enough, if you try harder, if you are more patient, things will change. Faith is powerful, but faith is not foolishness. You can believe in God and still walk away from danger. Sometimes obedience looks like leaving.

When I finally left my abusive marriage, I was terrified. I did not have money. I did not have stability. I did not have a plan that made sense on paper. What I had was three children and a breaking point.

Fear will tell you that you cannot make it on your own. Fear will tell you that it will get worse if you leave. Fear will tell you that no one else will want you. Fear is loud, but it is not always honest.

You are stronger than you think you are.

That strength does not show up all at once. It shows up in small decisions. It shows up when you say, "This is not okay." It shows up when you pack a bag. It shows up when you ask for help. It shows up when you choose peace over pride.

There is also something else I want you to understand: being alone is not the worst thing that can happen to you. Being mistreated while calling it love is worse.

Loneliness can be healed. Abuse leaves scars that take years to untangle.

Do not rush into a relationship because you are tired of being by yourself. Do not ignore red flags because you are afraid of starting over. Red flags do not turn green with time. They turn into patterns.

Look at how he handles frustration. Look at how he talks about other women. Look at how he speaks to his mother. Look at whether he keeps his word. Watch the small things. The small things are previews of the big ones.

And if you come from a background like mine, where chaos felt normal, you may have to retrain your mind. Peace might feel boring. Stability might feel unfamiliar. You might even mistake calm for a lack of passion. That is trauma talking.

Healthy love does not make your heart race out of fear. It makes your life steadier.

When I met a man who respected me, who did not yell, who did not threaten, who did not try to own me, I did not trust it at first. I was waiting for the explosion. I was waiting for the mask to fall. I had to learn that not all men were the same. I had to learn that my past did not have to predict my future.

You can learn too.

Here is something else I want you to know: you are not responsible for fixing a broken man.

You are not a rehabilitation center. You are not a counselor. You are not a punching bag for someone else's trauma. If he refuses to grow, you cannot love him into maturity. Love is not meant to be a rescue mission.

And please understand this clearly: physical abuse is not the only kind of abuse.

There is emotional abuse. Constant criticism. Humiliation disguised as jokes. Threats disguised as concern. Isolation disguised as protection. Financial control disguised as leadership.

If you feel smaller every year you are with someone, pay attention. You should be growing in a healthy relationship, not disappearing.

Also, learn to love yourself outside of who you are dating. Build skills. Work. Save money. Develop your own identity. Dependence can trap you in places you should have left long ago. When you know you can stand on your own, you choose love from strength, not desperation.

And finally, if you are already in something unhealthy and you are reading this quietly, hoping no one sees, hear me.

It is not too late. You are not stupid for staying. You are not weak for being afraid. You are not foolish for loving someone who hurt you. But you do not have to stay where you are breaking.

Make a plan. Tell someone safe. Seek resources. Call family. Go to a shelter if you must. Pride cannot protect you. Silence will not save you.

I lived in abandoned houses. I rode buses before sunrise. I worked long shifts and locked my children inside because I had no other option. It was hard. It was exhausting. It was humiliating at times.

But it was still better than being beaten. It was still better than living every day on edge. It was still better than teaching my children that fear was normal.

You deserve peace. You deserve respect. You deserve a love that does not require you to shrink. And if you do not have that yet, choose yourself until you find it.

Lesson from the Storm:

Love should feel safe. If it does not, it is not love. Do not let fear keep you in places that are breaking you. Sometimes faith looks like staying. Sometimes faith looks like walking away. Learn the difference, and have the courage to choose life.

SECTION II

THE STORMS OF GRIEF

CHAPTER 5

When Disaster Strikes

Two weeks before my son died, I noticed the light leave his eyes.

It wasn't dramatic. There was no announcement. No explosion. Just a quiet shift that only a mother would catch. He moved through the house differently; slower and quieter. Present in body, but not fully there in spirit. I watched him from the kitchen one evening while he leaned against the counter, staring at nothing in particular, and something in my chest tightened.

He had just turned twenty-one on January first. A milestone birthday. I remember teasing him about being grown now, about how he thought twenty-one made him a full man overnight. He laughed that laugh of his, wide and boyish, but I could see he felt the weight of adulthood pressing down on him. He was a young father. He was trying to handle responsibilities that felt bigger than his years. He wanted to prove he could stand on his own.

He had heartbreak too. A relationship falling apart. Tension over seeing his child. The kind of pressure that makes a young man feel like he has to hold everything together by himself. He did not want to worry me. He had said that more than once.

One night, I came home from work after a long shift. Twelve hours. Maybe sixteen. The house was quiet when I walked in, but not peaceful. The kind of quiet that hums with something underneath it. I dropped my purse on the table and saw him sitting there, elbows on his knees, head bowed.

At first I thought he was tired.

Then I saw the tears.

They slid off his face silently, landing on his jeans. He didn't even look up when I walked closer.

"What's wrong?" I asked, kneeling beside him. "Talk to me."

He wiped his face quickly like he could erase what I had already seen. "Mama, I didn't want to worry you."

Those seven words echo in my mind even now. I didn't want to worry you.

He told me he was frustrated. Hurt. He felt like he was failing as a father. He felt stuck. I rubbed his back and told him what mothers always say. "You don't have to carry everything alone. I'm here. You can talk to me about anything."

I believed that was enough.

I did not know about the new friends he had started spending time with. I did not know about the late-night conversations or the different tone in his voice when he came home. I did not know about what they called "water."

Later, I learned that "water" was not harmless. It was cigarettes or marijuana dipped in PCP or embalming fluid. A drug that distorts reality. A drug that makes shadows move and voices whisper. A drug that can send a mind somewhere the body cannot follow.

People saw him using. They noticed changes. They saw the confusion in his eyes. But they said he did not want to worry me.

Everyone protected my peace. Except my son.

The night he told me he was seeing things, his voice shook. His eyes darted around the room like something invisible was chasing him.

"Mama, I keep seeing stuff," he said. "I can't make it stop."

"What are you seeing?" I asked, trying to stay calm even though my heart had started pounding.

"Demons. Shadows. Stuff crawling on the walls."

His breathing was shallow. His hands trembled. I grabbed his face gently, trying to anchor him to me.

"There's nothing there," I whispered. "You're safe. I'm here."

But he wasn't looking at me. He was looking past me. Through me. Into a world I could not see.

I prayed out loud that night. I held him. I told him everything would be okay. I did not know he was already fighting a battle inside his own mind.

On the day he died, I was away at a seminar for work. It was an ordinary morning. People were talking about schedules and presentations. Coffee cups clinked against saucers. Pens scratched against paper. Nothing in the air warned me.

Then my phone rang.

When I answered, I heard screaming. Confusion. Voices overlapping. Someone finally said the words that split my life in two.

"There's been a shooting."

My body went cold. Not the kind of cold you feel in winter. The kind that starts in your chest and spreads outward like ice water pouring through your veins. I could not breathe. I grabbed my bag and ran for my car, dialing numbers, praying, begging.

"Lord, please. Please. Not my baby."

As I turned onto my street, I saw flashing red and blue lights bouncing off the houses. Neighbors stood in clusters along the sidewalk. Yellow tape cut across my yard like a line drawn between before and after.

I jumped out of the car and ran.

"That's my son! That's my baby!"

An officer caught me before I reached the yard. His grip was firm, but I fought him with everything in me. "Let me go! Let me see him!"

For a moment, he loosened his hold just enough for me to look past him.

My son was lying on the ground.

Still.

The world around him moved. Officers walked. Neighbors whispered. Lights flashed. But he did not move.

His face was calm. Not twisted. Not afraid.

Calm, and he was smiling.

Smiling.

It did not make sense. Nothing made sense. I heard someone explaining that he had been hallucinating, that he thought something was attacking him, that he had been shooting at what he believed were demons. They said it was the drug. They said it distorted his mind. They said he did not understand what he was doing.

Their words sounded far away, like I was underwater and someone was speaking from the surface.

In that moment, I heard him. Not with my ears; with my spirit.

"Mama, I'm all right."

My knees buckled. The officer held me up as my body gave way. I do not remember screaming. I do not remember falling. I remember silence. A strange, heavy silence that swallowed everything.

Two days after his twenty-first birthday.

My baby was gone.

The rest of that day came in fragments. Police questions. Papers to sign. Family arriving with swollen eyes. Someone holding my shoulders while I stared at nothing. I moved through it like a ghost inside my own life.

That night, I walked through the house and felt like I had stepped into a stranger's home. His shoes were still by the door. His jacket hung over a chair. The television remote sat where he had left it. Every object felt like a reminder that life had not been warned.

I stood in his doorway and stared at the empty bed. I kept expecting him to come down the hallway. To hear him say, "Mama," the way he always did when he needed something.

Instead, there was silence.

The days that followed felt like walking underwater. I could see people talking to me, but their voices sounded distant and distorted. I answered when spoken to. I went to work. I fed my other children. I paid bills. On the outside, I was functioning.

On the inside, I was unraveling. Some mornings, I could not get out of bed. My legs felt heavy, like grief had weight and was pressing me into the mattress.

I would stare at the ceiling and feel nothing and everything at the same time.

Sometimes in the dark, I whispered, "Lord, take me too."

Not because I wanted to die in a dramatic way. But because I did not know how to live in a world where my son did not exist. Half of me felt missing, and I did not know how to find the rest.

CHAPTER 6

From Disaster to Tragedy

Some storms come once, tear your world apart, and leave you standing in wreckage you never expected to see. You spend years trying to rebuild, trying to breathe normally again, trying to convince your heart that it is safe to hope. You tell yourself lightning does not strike the same place twice.

But sometimes it does.

It was early when the phone rang. Still dark outside. The kind of quiet hour when the world has not fully woken up. I was getting dressed for work, moving through my normal routine, when my phone lit up beside me. I almost let it ring twice before answering.

On the other end was my daughter-in-law, and her voice did not sound right.

"He's having bad stomach pain," she said. "We're taking him to an urgent clinic."

Stomach pain. That did not sound like danger. It sounded uncomfortable. It sounded temporary. I had heard him mention it before in passing. A little pain. A little discomfort. The kind of thing you think will pass.

Still, something about her tone made me pause.

A few minutes later, she called again. This time the fear was louder.

"They're sending us somewhere else," she said. "They think something's wrong."

I could hear movement in the background. Doors opening. Nurses speaking quickly. My heart began to beat harder, but my mind resisted panic. People go to the hospital every day. People have procedures. People come home.

Then she put a doctor on the phone.

The doctor's voice was professional but urgent. They were talking about internal bleeding. They were talking about low blood levels. They were talking about not having the right equipment. They might need to airlift him to a larger hospital.

Airlift.

That word did not fit with stomach pain.

I remember standing in my bedroom half-dressed, trying to process how a normal morning had turned into something heavy. I threw on my clothes with shaking hands and grabbed my keys.

"Lord, please," I whispered. "Just let me get there."

On the drive, my mind kept arguing with what I was hearing. He is young. He is strong. This is going to be fine. I kept repeating that like it was a promise.

Then the phone rang again.

This time, there was no steady voice. Only crying.

I heard words that did not belong together. He's not responding. They're trying. It's bad. It's really bad.

"No," I said out loud in my car. "No. That doesn't make sense."

I drove faster.

When I reached the hospital, the air inside felt cold and clinical. The smell of disinfectant hit me first. I followed the sound of hurried footsteps and muffled voices until I reached the room.

Doctors and nurses surrounded the bed.

Machines beeped.

Someone was pressing on his chest.

Someone else was shouting numbers.

The room felt crowded, but I felt alone inside it. Like my spirit had stepped back from my body to protect itself from what it was seeing.

My daughter was crying near the wall. My daughter-in-law stood frozen, hands clasped together like she was holding on to hope with her fingers.

I walked closer to the bed slowly, like moving too fast would make it real.

They were doing CPR.

My son's body moved with each push against his chest. Not because he was breathing. Because they were forcing him to.

"Come on," someone said. "Stay with us."

I wanted to say the same thing. Stay with us. Stay with me. But the words stuck in my throat.

Then everything slowed. The beeping changed. The room shifted. A doctor stepped back, looked at the clock, and then looked at me.

"I'm so sorry," the doctor said.

The words fell heavy into the air. I shook my head automatically. No. No. No. That is not what this morning was supposed to be. He had only come in with stomach pain. People do not die from stomach pain.

I walked to the bed and touched his face. His skin was warm but already different. I kissed his cheek, hoping for a response. Hoping for a twitch. A breath. A miracle.

Nothing moved. My second son was gone.

The shock was different this time. When I lost my first son, it felt like the ground had dropped from under me. This time, it felt like the sky collapsed on top of me.

I had already buried one child. I had already stood over a casket once. I had already felt that ripping sensation in my chest. I thought that kind of pain was rare. Singular.

Now I was standing in another hospital room facing the same nightmare.

What made it even harder was that just days before, we had been laughing.

He had come by the house riding his horse. He loved that horse. When he rode, he sat tall in the saddle like he belonged there. He came down the street fast, smiling like life was wide open in front of him.

I stood in the yard watching him, pretending to fuss.

"Slow down," I called out, though I was smiling.

He laughed and circled back around, dust kicking up under the hooves. The sound of metal against pavement echoed down the block. Neighbors peeked out their windows to watch.

He talked about the Houston Rodeo Parade like it was the biggest event in the world. He wanted new boots. A fresh pair of jeans. He wanted to ride downtown looking sharp.

If you know Houston, you know that parade is more than just a ride. It is tradition. Streets close. Crowds gather early with folding chairs and coolers. Marching bands fill the air with music. Horses line up in rows. Leather saddles shine under the sun. You can hear the rhythm of hooves hitting pavement long before you see them turn the corner.

He wanted to be part of that.

"I'm going to be out there," he told me. "You better be watching."

"I'll be there," I said.

I did not know that would be one of the last times I saw him smile like that.

He never made it to the parade.

Back in that hospital room, I felt like time had betrayed me. Just days earlier, he had been strong and alive and dreaming out loud. Now I was standing beside a still body that looked like it was just sleeping.

The ride home from the hospital was silent. I do not remember who drove. I only remember staring out of the window at streets that looked exactly the same as they had that morning.

How could the world look normal when mine had just shattered again?

When I walked into my house, it felt like déjà vu. The same heaviness. The same hollow echo in the rooms. The same disbelief that I would never hear his footsteps again: two sons, two graves. A pain that does not divide but multiplies.

That night, I did not scream. I did not collapse the way I had the first time. I sat on the edge of my bed and stared at the wall. My body felt tired beyond exhaustion. My heart felt like it had been cracked open twice and stitched back together without anesthesia.

I remember whispering, "Lord, I cannot do this again."

But it had already happened. The storm had returned, and I was standing in it.

CHAPTER 7

Learning to Breathe Again

After the second funeral, the world did not look different, but it felt different. The same streets were there. The same bills still showed up. The same calendar kept flipping days like nothing had happened. That was one of the cruelest parts of grief to me. Life keeps moving like it never got the memo that your heart just broke again.

The quiet in my house became heavy. It was not peaceful quiet. It was not the kind that helps you rest. It was the kind that sits in the corners of rooms and presses against your chest. I would walk from one room to another and feel like the air itself was thicker. Sometimes I would stand still in the hallway, not because I had something to do there, but because my body forgot where it was going. Grief can do that. It interrupts your thinking, steals your focus, and turns simple routines into chores that take all your strength.

People talk about time like it is a healer, but time does not heal. Time just keeps moving. The sun rises. The phone rings. Somebody needs something. A meal still needs to be cooked. Work still expects you to show up. Life continues to demand function from you while you feel like you are barely holding yourself together. I learned that grief does not pause your responsibilities. If anything, it makes them heavier because you have to carry normal life on top of abnormal pain.

There were days I would start a task and forget what I was doing halfway through it. I would open a cabinet and just stare, trying to remember what I came for. My mind felt like it was covered in fog. I would lose track of time, lose track of conversations, lose track of myself. At night, sleep would not come easy. When it did, it did not feel like rest. I would wake up tired, like grief had been working my body all night while I was trying to lay still.

My thoughts turned into replay. The phone calls. The hospital rooms. The sound of "I'm so sorry." The images came back without warning. Sometimes it would happen in the grocery store aisle. Sometimes in the car at a red light. Sometimes in the middle of laughter, when a grandchild said something funny and joy tried to rise, but sorrow rose right behind it. I could smile and still feel that ache underneath, because two things can live in the same heart at the same time.

Then the questions started, the kind that do not have answers but still show up like they deserve one. What if I had insisted on a different clinic? What if I had gotten there sooner? What if I had asked more questions when he first said his stomach hurt? What if I had seen something earlier? What if… what if… what if. Those questions can torture you if you let them, because they keep you reaching for control you never really had.

Some days it was not sadness that rose up first. Some days it was anger. Anger at the unfairness of it. Anger at the timing. Anger at the fact that I had already survived this once and now it was happening again. I did not always know where to put the anger, and when you do not have a place to put it, it can turn into guilt. Guilt has a quiet voice, but it knows how to stay. It whispers that you should have prevented it, that you missed something, that you failed.

A mother's heart does not stop wanting to protect her children just because they grow up. That instinct stays. When they are grown, you still want to fix what hurts them. You still want to take the pain off of them and put it on yourself. You still want to stand between them and harm. So when harm comes anyway, the question becomes personal even if it is not logical. You start wondering what you could have done differently, and grief starts mixing with self-blame.

I had to wrestle with that in private, because a lot of people do not know what to say to a mother who has buried two sons. They offer what they can. They say, "Be strong." They say, "God knows best." They say, "They're in a better place." I understood their intentions, but I needed something deeper than phrases. I needed space to tell the truth without being rushed, corrected, or preached at like my pain was a lack of faith.

Strength did not look like standing tall during that season. Strength looked like getting out of bed when my body felt glued to the mattress. Strength looked like putting my feet on the floor even when my legs felt weak. Strength looked like brushing my hair, washing my face, and showing up to work with a smile that felt like it belonged to somebody else. Strength looked like coming home, fixing something to eat, and still making sure the people who were alive in my house felt loved.

There were moments when I felt detached from everything, even from joy. Grandchildren would run through the room laughing, and I would smile because I loved them, but part of me would be thinking, They should be here to see this. They should be holding their babies. They should be laughing right along with them. That thought would arrive out of nowhere and sit on my chest like weight. It did not mean I was ungrateful.

It meant I was grieving what was missing even while I was appreciating what remained.

Grief also changed my body. I felt tired in ways that sleep did not fix. My shoulders felt heavy as if I had been carrying something invisible. My breathing sometimes felt shallow, like my lungs did not want to make room for all that pain. Some mornings I sat on the edge of the bed and stared at my hands, talking myself into movement. I would whisper, "Get up. You still got life in you." That became a kind of prayer, not fancy, not loud, but honest.

My faith changed too. It became less about the kind of faith that speaks in church voice and more about the kind of faith that whispers through tears. I did not always have big prayers during that time. Some nights all I had was one sentence. "Lord, help me." Other nights it was, "Lord, hold me." Sometimes it was just, "Lord…," and nothing else came out after it. I learned that God does not require perfect words. He responds to real ones.

I also learned that grieving two children is not the same as grieving one child twice. Each loss has its own shape. Each one carries its own memories. Each one brings up its own questions. A mother's love is not measured or divided. It is full. It is whole. So when one child is gone, the empty space is specific. When two are gone, the silence doubles, and the heart has to learn how to hold two absences at once.

During that season, I started writing again, not because I was trying to create something for the world, but because I needed a place to put what was inside of me. My body could not hold all that pain without cracking. Sometimes the writing was messy. Sometimes it was just a sentence. Sometimes it was a memory. Sometimes it was anger. Sometimes it was questions I did not have answers for. But getting it out of my chest and onto paper helped me breathe.

That is what grief forced me to learn. Breathing again is not one big moment. It is a series of small decisions. It is choosing to take a shower. Choosing to answer the phone. Choosing to go outside. Choosing to eat something even when food tastes like nothing. Choosing to sit with family even when you feel like a ghost among the living. Most people do not call those things victory, but I learned they are.

Grief did not leave me. It changed shape. At first it was sharp and constant, like I was being cut open every day. Later it became quieter, but it never disappeared. It turned into waves instead of a flood, but waves can still knock you down if you are not prepared. A song in the store. A familiar scent. A holiday. A birthday. A quiet Sunday morning. Those were the moments when grief would hit again, hard and sudden, reminding me that love does not disappear just because someone does.

I learned that grief is not something you "get over." It is something you learn to live with. It becomes a part of you, not to destroy you, but to deepen you. It makes you softer in some places, stronger in others, more present, more aware of what matters. It teaches you that life is fragile, and love is sacred, and time is not promised.

There were mornings I would look in the mirror and barely recognize the woman staring back at me. Her eyes looked older. There was wisdom there, but there was also weariness. I would speak to myself like I was speaking to someone I loved, because I needed that tenderness. I would say, "You still here." Some days that was the only truth I could hold.

I did not have all the answers. I still do not. I could not explain why I survived what I survived. I could not explain why my sons did not get to stay. But I knew I had a choice in how I would live after it. I could let grief swallow what was left of me, or I could fight, slowly and imperfectly, to stay present for the life still in front of me.

That fight did not look dramatic. It looked like showing up. It looked like breathing when breathing felt heavy. It looked like learning how to live again, one small decision at a time.

CHAPTER 8

The Day I Chose to Live

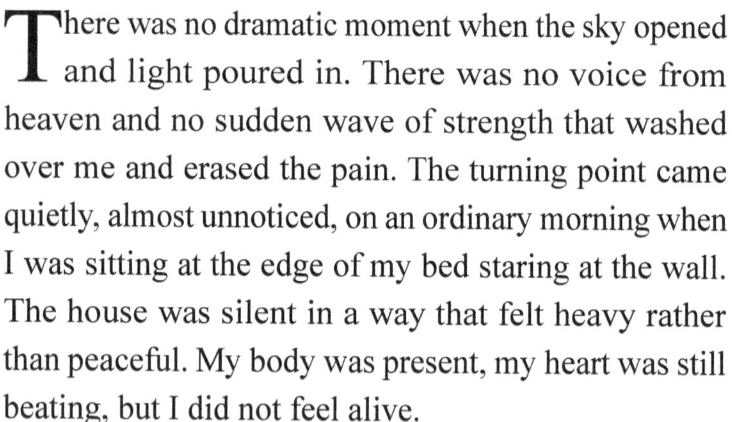

There was no dramatic moment when the sky opened and light poured in. There was no voice from heaven and no sudden wave of strength that washed over me and erased the pain. The turning point came quietly, almost unnoticed, on an ordinary morning when I was sitting at the edge of my bed staring at the wall. The house was silent in a way that felt heavy rather than peaceful. My body was present, my heart was still beating, but I did not feel alive.

That morning, I asked myself a question I had been avoiding for months: *Am I going to die while I am still living?* Grief had already taken so much from me. It had taken my sons. It had taken my energy. It had taken my focus and parts of my laughter. Slowly, almost without me noticing, it had begun reaching for the rest of me. I realized I was allowing it to.

There is a difference between honoring grief and surrendering to it. For a long time, I could not tell the difference. I believed that staying wrapped in sorrow proved how much I loved my sons. I believed that smiling again would mean I was forgetting them. I believed that moving forward would mean leaving them behind. None of that was true. Love does not disappear when you begin living again. Love does not fade because you choose to breathe deeply.

As I sat there that morning, I looked around my room and saw reminders that life was still unfolding around me. Grandchildren still laughed. Family members still called. Responsibilities still required my hands and my voice. I understood something simple but powerful: I was still here. If I was still here, then my story was not finished.

I did not wake up feeling strong. I woke up exhausted. Still, I made a small decision. I swung my legs off the bed, stood up, and walked to the bathroom. When I looked at my reflection, I did not see the woman I used to be. I saw someone older, someone marked by loss, someone carrying weight. But I also saw someone who had survived. I spoke out loud to that reflection and said, "You are not done." The words felt unfamiliar, but they were necessary.

For months, grief had become my atmosphere. I carried it into every room. I expected every day to feel heavy, and because I expected it, I allowed it to settle deeper. That morning, I realized that choosing to live did not mean choosing to forget. It meant choosing to carry my sons with me instead of collapsing beside their absence. It meant honoring them by continuing to move.

The shift was not emotional. It was disciplined. I began setting small goals that felt almost too simple to matter. I would wake up and make my bed. I would step outside for fresh air. I would call someone instead of isolating myself. I would write when my thoughts felt overwhelming instead of letting them spiral. I would pray even when my words felt dry. Each small action felt like resistance against the heaviness that had tried to claim me.

Grief did not disappear. It still arrived without warning. It still brought waves of memory and moments of ache. But I stopped giving it permanent residence. When sadness rose, I let myself feel it without allowing it to take control of the entire day. I began to understand that waves pass when you do not fight them or drown in them.

One afternoon, I was watching my grandchildren play in the yard. One of them laughed so hard that they fell backward into the grass. The sound was loud, bright, and free. For a brief moment, joy rose in me without hesitation. Instead of pushing it away, I allowed it to stay. That small moment taught me something important: my heart was still capable of expansion. Pain had not sealed it shut.

Living again did not mean I stopped missing my sons. It meant I stopped allowing their absence to steal every present moment. I began speaking about them without collapsing. I began sharing stories that carried warmth instead of only tears. I began to understand that remembering them with strength was not betrayal. It was honor.

I also recognized that people were watching me, even when they did not say so. My children were watching to see how their mother would stand after being knocked down twice. My grandchildren were watching to see whether sorrow would silence me. Others who had experienced loss were watching quietly, wondering if survival was possible. I did not want the lesson of my life to be that storms win.

That realization strengthened my resolve. I had survived poverty. I had survived abuse. I had survived heartbreak. I had survived burying one son, and then another. Survival had followed me through every chapter of my life. It was not accidental. It was evidence that something greater had been carrying me all along.

My faith changed during that season. It became less about polished prayers and more about honest conversation. Some days my prayers were nothing more than, "Lord, help me keep going." Other days they were quiet acknowledgments that I did not understand His ways but trusted His presence. I stopped trying to sound strong and started being real. That honesty deepened my relationship with God more than any perfect prayer ever had.

Purpose slowly began to replace paralysis. I started to see that my experiences were not only wounds; they were testimony. The girl who once lived in an abandoned house. The woman who walked away from abuse. The mother who buried two sons yet still stood. That is not a story of defeat. It is a story of endurance.

The day I chose to live was not dramatic. There were no fireworks or applause. It was a quiet commitment made in a bedroom that had held too many tears. It was a decision to breathe deeply, to show up fully, to love fiercely, and to speak honestly. It was a decision to live intentionally, not because the pain was gone, but because I was still here.

Choosing life did not remove the scars. It gave them meaning. It allowed me to see that storms can shape you without stopping you. They can bend you without breaking you. They can deepen your faith, widen your compassion, and strengthen your resolve.

That morning, when I stood in front of the mirror and said, "You are not done," I was not declaring victory over grief. I was declaring partnership with life. I was choosing to walk forward with sorrow in one hand and hope in the other. I was deciding that what remained in me was stronger than what had been taken from me.

And from that quiet decision, everything began to change.

CHAPTER 9

Life After the Storm

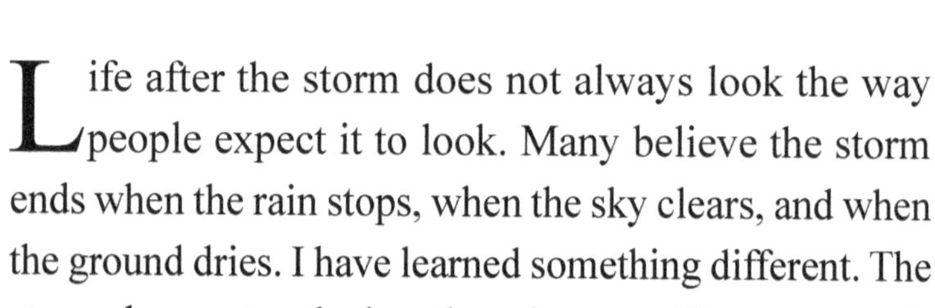

Life after the storm does not always look the way people expect it to look. Many believe the storm ends when the rain stops, when the sky clears, and when the ground dries. I have learned something different. The storm does not end when the rain stops. The storm ends when you learn how to stand confidently in the rain.

For a long time, I thought healing would mean the pain disappearing completely. I believed there would be a day when I would wake up and feel nothing but peace. I imagined a version of life where grief no longer visited, where memories did not sting, where tears no longer surprised me. That day never came.

What came instead was strength.

The rain still falls sometimes. There are days when memories rise suddenly. There are moments when a song, a smell, or a date on the calendar brings tears to my eyes. There are quiet evenings when I miss my sons so deeply that my chest tightens. That has not changed.

What has changed is me.

I no longer collapse when the rain begins. I no longer panic when sadness visits. I no longer interpret tears as weakness. I understand now that crying does not mean I am drowning. It means I loved deeply.

Life after the storm is not about dryness. It is about steadiness.

There was a time when every emotional wave knocked me down. Now, when grief rises, I let it move through me without letting it carry me away. I stand in it. I breathe through it. I trust that it will pass. I have learned the difference between feeling pain and being controlled by pain.

That is freedom.

I used to brace myself whenever something unexpected happened. If the phone rang late at night, my heart would race. If someone I loved was delayed, my mind would spiral toward worst-case scenarios. Loss had trained me to expect disaster. But living in constant anticipation of tragedy is another kind of prison.

At some point, I made a decision that fear would not narrate my life. I cannot control everything that happens, but I can control how I respond. I refuse to spend today worrying about what may or may not come tomorrow.

That decision changed the way I move through the world.

I love openly again. I speak honestly again. I laugh freely again. I allow joy to exist without apologizing for it. There was a season when happiness felt like betrayal, as if smiling meant I had forgotten my sons. I now understand that joy honors them. Living well is not disrespectful to those we have lost. It is a continuation of the love we shared with them.

Life after the storm has given me a different kind of confidence. It is not loud or boastful. It is quiet and rooted. I know what I have survived. I know what tried to take me out. I know the nights I cried until I had nothing left in me. I also know that I woke up the next morning anyway.

That knowledge changes a person.

When challenges come now, I do not immediately crumble. I pause. I breathe. I remember. I remind myself that I have already survived what I once thought was impossible. That memory strengthens me. It gives me perspective. It tells me that this new obstacle, whatever it is, does not have more power than the storms I have already endured.

There is authority in survival.

I no longer see myself as the woman tragedy followed. I see myself as the woman who endured and remained. My identity is not rooted in what happened to me, but in how I rose after it happened. That shift in identity is life after the storm.

My faith has deepened in ways I cannot fully explain. I no longer measure God's presence by whether life is easy. I measure it by whether I am sustained. In hospital rooms, He sustained me. In dark bedrooms, He sustained me. In funerals and in silence, He sustained me. Life after the storm has shown me that His faithfulness does not disappear when the clouds gather.

Because of that, I do not fear clouds the way I once did.

I understand now that rain does not automatically mean destruction. Sometimes rain cleanses. Sometimes it softens hardened ground. Sometimes it nourishes growth that cannot happen in dry seasons. Pain, while unwelcome, has refined me. It has made me more compassionate, more patient, more aware of the fragility of life.

I notice things now that I once rushed past. The sound of grandchildren laughing in the next room. The warmth of sunlight on my face. The quiet peace of an ordinary afternoon. I do not take those moments for granted. Loss sharpened my gratitude.

Life after the storm is not perfect. It is purposeful.

There are still tears. There are still memories. There are still days when I sit quietly and speak my sons' names in prayer. But there is also laughter. There is stability. There is strength. There is peace that coexists with sorrow.

That coexistence is maturity.

I stand in the rain now without fear that it will sweep me away. I stand knowing that I have weathered worse. I stand knowing that I bend but do not break. I stand knowing that my foundation is stronger than any storm that comes against it.

Victory is not the absence of rain. Victory is standing steady while it falls.

When people ask me how I made it through, I do not give them a complicated answer. I tell them I kept breathing. I kept praying. I kept choosing to rise, even when rising felt heavy. I allowed myself to feel without surrendering to despair. I trusted that my life still had meaning, even when it felt shattered.

Life after the storm is not about pretending the storm never happened. It is about carrying its lessons forward without carrying its weight forever.

I am not untouched. I am transformed.

The rain still comes. But now, when it does, I lift my face instead of hiding. I let it fall. I let it remind me that I am still here.

And I stand.

CHAPTER 10

What I Want You to Know

If you have read this far, then you have walked with me through some of the hardest chapters of my life. You have stood in hospital rooms with me. You have sat in silence with me. You have felt the weight of loss, the confusion of grief, and the slow climb back toward hope. Before we close this book, there are a few things I want you to know.

First, storms do not mean you are weak. They do not mean you lack faith. They do not mean you did something wrong. Life brings rain to every house. Some storms are brief. Others linger. Some shake your windows. Others tear the roof off. But none of them are proof that you are incapable. If anything, they are proof that you are human.

Second, grief is not a straight line. It does not move neatly from pain to peace. It circles back. It revisits. It surprises you. There will be days when you feel strong and days when you feel fragile. Both are normal. Both are allowed. Strength does not mean you never cry. Strength means you cry and continue.

I want you to know that you are allowed to feel everything. Anger. Confusion. Sadness. Fear. Do not rush your healing to make other people comfortable. Do not silence your pain because someone else thinks it has been long enough. Healing is not measured by the calendar. It is measured by honesty.

If you are a parent carrying guilt, release it. You are not all-knowing. You are not all-powerful. You loved with the information you had at the time. That is what mothers and fathers do. Do not let "what if" steal the years you still have left. Guilt will try to convince you that you could have controlled everything. That is not truth. That is torment.

If you are battling depression, speak. Do not suffer in silence. Silence grows heavy. It isolates you. There is no shame in asking for help. There is no weakness in counseling. There is no failure in needing support. Strength includes reaching out. Strength includes admitting you cannot carry it alone.

If you are standing in the middle of your own storm right now, I want you to remember this: you have survived every hard day up to this one. That is not accidental. There is resilience inside you that you may not even recognize yet. Even if all you can do today is breathe and get through the next hour, that is enough.

I want you to understand that life after loss is still life. It may look different. It may feel different. You may never be the same person you were before the storm. But different does not mean destroyed. Different can mean deeper. Wiser. More compassionate. More aware of what truly matters.

You do not have to pretend that everything is fine. You do not have to put on a strong face for the world. You can be honest about your scars and still walk with dignity. Your scars are not evidence of failure. They are evidence that you endured.

I also want you to know that joy is not betrayal. Smiling again does not mean you have forgotten the people you loved. Laughing does not mean you are insensitive to what you lost. Joy and grief can sit in the same heart. You can miss someone deeply and still enjoy the life in front of you. That balance is not disrespectful. It is healthy.

There will be days when the rain returns. Anniversaries. Birthdays. Unexpected reminders. When those days come, do not panic. Let the tears fall if they need to. Let the memories surface. Feel them. Honor them. Then stand again. You are not starting over each time you cry. You are continuing.

Faith may look different for you now than it once did. That is not failure; it is growth. Faith that has been tested is not fragile. It is refined. You may not have all the answers, and that is okay. Sometimes faith is simply choosing to trust that there is purpose even when you cannot see it.

I want you to guard your heart but not close it. Pain can tempt you to build walls so high that nothing else can get in. But walls that keep pain out also keep love out. Keep your heart open. Love again. Dream again. Hope again. Life is too precious to live in permanent fear of what might happen.

If my story has taught you anything, I hope it has shown you that storms do not get the final word. They may shape you, but they do not define you. They may bend you, but they do not have to break you. There is strength in you that you may not discover until it is tested. When it is tested, do not run from it. Rise into it.

You are stronger than you think. You are more resilient than you feel. You are more supported than you realize. Even in your darkest moments, you are not invisible. You are not forgotten. You are not alone.

Guard your faith. Feed your hope. Protect your peace. Speak your truth. Cry when you need to. Rest when you must. Stand when you can.

Remember this above all: no matter how fierce the wind has been or how long the rain has fallen, the storm was never meant to be your home. You are strong enough to travel *Through Life's Storms*.